CARRY-OUT
DIFFICULT TASK FIRST

Doing The Hard Things First To
Achieve Greater Goals

JACK COLLINS

DISCLAIMER

This book is only intended to provide knowledge that is relevant to daily life. Every effort has been made to provide accurate, current, trustworthy, and comprehensive information.It is important to note that the information provided is intended for educational and informational purposes only.

Table of contents

INTRODUCTION

Carrying out difficult tasks can frequently be daunting and inviting, but there are several reasons why it's a good idea to attack them first. Originally, by completing difficult tasks beforehand, you can avoid procrastinating and putting them off, which can lead to added stress and anxiety. Secondly, completing difficult tasks can give you a sense of accomplishment and motivation to continue with the rest of your tasks. Eventually, if you leave difficult tasks until the end of the day, you may find that you're too tired or have run out of time to complete them to the stylish of your capability. Thus, by prioritizing difficult tasks, you can ensure that they admit the attention and concentration they bear, eventually leading to a more productive and successful outgrowth.

CHAPTER 1

REASONS WHY YOU CARRY- OUT DIFFICULT TASKS LAST.

People choose to complete easier tasks first not on the logical basis of what methodology is more productive, but on what system makes them feel more. lower tasks are generally easier to postpone, delegate, or avoid entirely than large tasks if time or motivation runs low. People have a limited quantum of energy in any given week to produce or perform. It's more productive to consider whether you need to perform small tasks at all rather than do them first. People performing small tasks tend to multitask, and multitasking isn't productive – it only feels productive. Completing lower tasks first is formative procrastination, and destroys productivity. Doing the hardest task first means you're more likely to complete it. Getting the hardest task out of the way allows you to seacoast and creates a positive mood, which increases productivity. It's important to attempt these tasks because you can make confidence for the coming attempts you'll make in the future to negotiate that thing. By going through or trying difficult tasks, you can gain a lot of knowledge and gain experience/ wisdom for the coming tasks you try to attempt. Often, avoidance of a difficult task is related to fear. This could be related to the fear of getting started, the fear of incapability to complete the task, or simply a fear of a lack of knowledge about the task. In all cases, fear leads to inactivity, which leads to a further lack of confidence. To indeed suffer change and growth, we need to step outside of our comfort zone. This is where all the magic happens. This is where we do the difficult tasks that we don't always want to do. As we do difficult effects more and more, they come lightly and more manageable. Anything most worthwhile literacy in life takes some difficulty and time to come complete. To achieve the effects you never have, you have to do the effects you have never done. How great do you want to be? Still, also your desire for growth may not be naturally motivating enough If this question makes you uncomfortable. You may need to have some confidence in your capacities to do the difficult tasks in the first place. Still, you first need to admit the fear that's holding you back, If you're going to be confident. Frequently, avoidance of difficult tasks is related to fear. This could be related to the fear of getting started, the fear of incapability to complete the task, or simply a fear of a lack of knowledge about the task. In all cases, fear leads to inactivity, which leads to a further lack of confidence. There are different reasons why people may choose to carry out difficult tasks last, and some of these reasons include:

1. Procrastination. Procrastination is a common argument why people may set off on difficult tasks until the last nanosecond. It's frequently easier and further tempting to concentrate on easier or further easier tasks first, leaving the further gruelling bones for later.

2. Lack of motivation. Some people may struggle to detect motivation to tackle difficult tasks. When tasks feel inviting, it can be gruelling to hail the dynamism and seat needed to get started.

3. Panic of failure. Difficult tasks can occasionally be associated with a panic of failure. However, they may set it off until the last nanosecond, hoping that

they will detect the courage or capability to do it later. If someone is hysterical they won't be suitable to complete a task or do it well.

4. Time operation. Penurious time operation can also contribute to putting off difficult tasks. People may give too important time on other tasks, leaving little time and dynamism for the further gruelling bones

In some cases, carrying out difficult tasks last may not be the stylish path, as it can lead to pressure, perturbation, and a rushed, deficient job. It may be better to break up the task down into a lower, more manageable corridor, and attack each portion. This can support instigation and confidence, making it easier to attack the further grueling aspects of the task.

CHAPTER 2

THE EXPERIENCE YOU GET WHEN YOU CARRY OUT DIFFICULT TASKS FIRST.

Serving the hard-bitten effects First is structured to save you time, boost internal dynamism, and educate you to suppose from a mindset erected with confidence by removing panic. You will learn how to concentrate on your task for the day, exclude devastation, and come up with a stylish interpretation of yourself in both your work and in life. No matter how bad your first trouble is, you'll be much happier for having made a launch. You'll have gotten off the blocks, started to get and understand what's demanded and you'll have made a mark on the proverbial empty distance. All of this will make you happier, especially if you've divided the hard-bitten stuff first. And once you start growing the task, it'll ultimately bend to your vagrancy, and you'll be rollicking with it like a puppy dog. Every time you shove yourself to do a difficult task, you'll grow your art set and you'll also grow as a person. The hard-bitten stuff is generally the important stuff but frequently not the critical stuff. It's constantly ready to set off serving the hard-bitten stuff, because in a lot of cases it'll be about your particular evolution. Indeed a difficult work task that's been assigned to you comes with evolution openings but failing to follow through and do the task has further counteraccusations than a lost excrescence occasion. Carrying out difficult tasks can be a precious literacy experience that can support you to grow and develop in colorful ways. These are some of the experiences you might gain from carrying out a difficult task.

1. Increased confidence. Completing a difficult task can give you a sense of accomplishment and boost your confidence. You may find that you are more willing to take on gruelling tasks in the future, knowing that you have the skills and determination to see them through.

2. Advanced problem working skills. Difficult tasks frequently bear you to suppose creatively and come up with innovative results for complex problems. This can ameliorate your capability to suppose

critically and problem-break effectively in other areas of your life.

3. Increased adaptability. Facing difficult challenges can also help you develop adaptability and perseverance. You may find that you are more equipped to handle lapses and challenges in the future, knowing that you've successfully overcome obstacles in history.

4. Advanced skills and knowledge. Difficult tasks frequently bear you to develop new skills or gain a deeper understanding of a particular subject. This can help you make your knowledge and moxie in a particular area, which can be precious in both particular and professional surroundings.

5. Personal growth. Eventually, carrying out difficult tasks can be a precious goal for personal growth and tone- discovery. You may find that you learn further about your strengths and sins, your heartstrings and interests, and your values and precedences. This tone- mindfulness can help you make better opinions and lead a further fulfilling life.

6. Resilience. When you attack difficult tasks, you're likely to encounter lapses and challenges. These experiences can help you develop adaptability and learn how to bounce back from failure.

7. Problem-solving skills. Difficult tasks frequently bear creative problem-solving skills. By working through gruelling problems, you can develop your capability to suppose critically and come up with innovative results.

8. Perseverance. Hard tasks frequently bear sustained trouble over some time. By persisting through Difficult tasks, you can develop your capability to stay focused and married to your goals.

9. Time-management skills. Difficult tasks can be time-consuming, and you may need to learn how to manage your time effectively to complete them. This can help you develop better time-management skills that can be applied to other areas of your life.

10. Self-confidence. Completing difficult tasks can give you a sense of accomplishment and boost your tone- confidence. This can help you feel more able and empowered in other areas of your life. Overall,

doing the hard task can be a gruelling but satisfying experience that can help you develop a range of skills and rates that are precious in both your personal and professional life.

CHAPTER 3

OVERCOMING FEAR AND REDUCING EXCUSES.

Think about your biggest thing. Why haven't you fulfilled it yet? For most people the answer is fear. Fear is the biggest factor stopping you from achieving your goals in life. Overcoming fear is one of the things you can do as a hobby. It's easy to pretend fear is not impacting you and to make excuses as to why you haven't achieved what you're able to. rather than turning around and hiding from it, treat fear as a cue to take action, not a reason. Fear generally causes procrastination by serving as an important emotional interference, which makes people more antipathetic to certain tasks, and causes those people to delay taking action as a way to delay whatever it's that they're hysterical of. For instance, if a person is hysterical about failing a task, they might also defer the task as a way to delay dealing with their fear.

Managing fear through this type of avoidance can help the plodder cover their mood in the short term, by helping them defer the thing that they're hysterical of. Still, in the long term, this generally hurts them further than it helps, for several reasons Procrastinating doesn't break the fear, but rather only postpones the point at which the plodder has to deal with it. Procrastinating can give the fear time to grow and come worse, which can increase the negative feelings associated with it. Procrastinating can give rise to new negative feelings, similar to frustration, guilt, and shame. you need to work on overcoming your fears. Because the less fearful you are, the less you'll hide behind excuses. However, you'll not only keep yourself from achieving your full goals, and stylish life, If you don't. You'll start believing so numerous excuses that there won't be any room left for creativity and threat in your life. You'll reduce your comfort zone until it fits in your fund. You'll come self- centered, and presumably veritably pessimistic. By counting on excuses you'll reject taking responsibility for your own life, and ultimately you'll presumably lament not having taken more chances in your life. Fear and excuses can frequently hold us back from achieving our goals and living our stylish lives. Fear can be a natural response to the unknown, but it can also become a limiting factor that prevents us from taking pitfalls and trying new tasks. Also, excuses are frequently used to avoid taking responsibility and making changes that we know are necessary. To overcome fear and excuses, it's important to identify the underpinning beliefs and allowed

patterns that are driving these actions. This may involve exploring your once confidence, seeking support from a therapist or counselor, or simply taking the time to reflect on your studies and passions. Once you've linked the root causes of your fear and excuses, you can begin to take action to overcome them. This might involve setting specific goals, breaking those goals down into lower ways, and taking action towards them regularly. You might also find it helpful to seek support from musketeers, family members, or a trainer who can give stimulants and responsibility. Remember that fear and excuses is a process, and it may not be overnight. Have patience with yourself and focus on achieving your goals. With time and trouble, you can learn to overcome your fears and take the conduct necessary to achieve your goals and live your stylish life. Overcoming fear and reducing excuses can be gruelling, but there are some strategies you can try

Step1.
Identify the source of your fear. Understanding what triggers your fear can help you come up with a plan to overcome it. For illustration, if you are hysterical about public speaking, you can start by rehearsing in front of a small group of people.

Step2.
Take a small way: Break down your thing into a lower, more manageable way. This can help you overcome fear and build confidence. For illustration, if you want to start exercising regularly, start by taking a walk around the block.

Step3.

Fantasize success. Picture yourself succeeding in your thing. This can help reduce anxiety and build confidence.

Step4.

Hold yourself responsible. Set specific, measurable goals and hold yourself responsible for them. Partake your goals with a friend or family member who can help keep you on track.

Step5.

Challenge your excuses. Identify the excuses you use to avoid taking action and challenge them. For illustration, if you are avoiding exercise because you do not have time, find ways to make time in your schedule, similar to waking up before or cutting back on other conditioning. Remember that overcoming fear and reducing excuses takes time and trouble. Be patient with yourself and be happy with your progress.

CHAPTER 4

GET RID OF LAZINESS AND

HOW TO OVERCOME LAZINESS.

Laziness is the desire to be idle, to do nothing, and to repel trouble. It's a state of passivity and of letting tasks stay as they are. Occasionally, we enjoy being a little lazy, similar to after working hard for several hours, or when we stay in bed on a veritably cold day. Still, if doing nothing occurs too frequently, something has to be done about it. You have to overcome laziness if you want to be successful and achieve a lot of things in life. Think about the benefits you'll gain if you overcome your laziness and take action, rather than allowing for difficulties or obstacles. fastening on the difficulties of carrying out the task, leads to despondency, avoidance of taking action and laziness. It's important that you concentrate your mind and attention on the benefits, not on the difficulties. Laziness is the tendency to avoid or repel doing work, plying trouble, or taking action. It can be caused by a lack of motivation, fear of failure, or feeling overwhelmed by a task. Laziness can be a gruelling habit to break, but it's possible with effort and the right strategies. There are some possible causes and effects of laziness

CAUSES
• Lack of motivation or interest in a task
• Fear of failure
• Low energy situations or physical fatigue
• Procrastination
• Negative thinking patterns
• Lack of clear goals or direction
• Unhealthy habits similar to increased screen time, lack of exercise, or poor sleep habits.

EFFECTS
• Missed opportunities
• Reduced productivity
• Poor performance at work or academy

• Low self-esteem
• Increased stress and anxiety
• Poor physical health due to lack of exercise or unhealthy habits
• simulated connections due to missed commitments or liabilities.

Still, it may be helpful to identify the underpinning causes and develop strategies to address them, If you're floundering with laziness. This may involve setting clear goals, creating a schedule, breaking tasks into lower levels, satisfying yourself, barring distractions, and changing your mindset. Remember that overcoming laziness takes time and trouble, but it's possible with continuity and the right approach.

HOW TO OVERCOME LAZINESS.

Overcoming laziness can be a difficult task, especially when it comes to carrying out difficult tasks. Still, there are several strategies that you can try to motivate yourself and push through the challenge.

Step1.

Break the task into a lower, more manageable way rather than looking at the task as a whole, break it down into a lower, attainable way. This can help you feel less overwhelmed and make it easier to get started.

Step2.

Set specific and attainable goals Set clear, attainable goals that are aligned with your overall ideal. This can help you stay focused and motivated as you work towards completing the task.

Step3.

Set a schedule or routine Set a specific time each day or week to work on the task, and stick to it. This can help you establish a routine and make the task feel more manageable.

Step4.

Exclude distractions Identify and exclude any distractions that may be precluding you from starting or completing the task. This may include turning off your phone or creating a quiet space to work.

Step5.

Find motivation Find a commodity that motivates you to complete the task, similar to a price or a sense of accomplishment. imagining the end result can also help you stay motivated and focused.

Step6.

Ask for help Do not be hysterical to ask for help if you need it. This can include asking a friend or coworker for support or advice or seeking out videos similar to tutorials or online forums.

Overcoming laziness takes time and hard work. Be patient, and do not be too hard on yourself if you witness lapses along the way.

CHAPTER 5

INCAPABILITY TO MAKE DECISION.

Decision-making is the ability to make choices. It involves assessing colorful factors, similar to the available information, possible issues, pitfalls and benefits, and particular values and preferences. Effective decision-making can have a significant impact on particular and professional success. incapability to make opinions can be a frustrating and gruelling experience. There are many implicit causes

• Fear of making the wrong decision. Occasionally, people may feel hysterical about making a decision because they worry about the implicit consequences.

• Lack of information. If you do not have enough information to make an informed decision, it can be difficult to move forward.

• Overwhelmed When faced with too many numerous options or considerations, it can be gruelling to decide.

• Analysis paralysis.
Occasionally, people may get stuck in a cycle of over-analyzing every option or script, which can lead to decision paralysis.

• Lack of confidence. If you warrant confidence in your capability to make opinions, it can be helpful to practice with lower opinions and make up for more significant opinions.

Incapability to make opinions when faced with difficult tasks can be a gruelling experience. Here are some tips that may help.

1. Break the task into lower, manageable parts. Divide the task into lower, more manageable parts. This will make the task feel less inviting and help you concentrate on one step at a time.

2. Identify the root of the problem. Take a moment to identify what's causing your indecisiveness. Is it a lack of information, fear of failure, or a sense of

overwhelm? Once you identify the root cause, you can develop strategies to overcome it.

3. Consider the consequences.
Consider the implicit consequences of not completing the task or delaying the decision. This can prompt you to take action.

4. Seek advice. Seek advice from trusted musketeers, family members, or professionals. Talking through the problem with someone differently can help you gain perspective and make a decision.

5. Set a deadline. Give yourself a deadline to make a decision and take action. Having a deadline can help you concentrate and overcome indecisiveness.

6. Fantasize success. Imagine the positive issues of completing the task or making the decision. This can help you feel more confident in your capability to succeed.

Remember that indecisiveness is a common experience, and it's possible to overcome it. With tolerance, self-reflection, and perseverance, you can develop the skills demanded to make difficult opinions and carry out gruelling tasks.

CHAPTER 6

FEAR OF CRITICISM.

Numerous people indeed have a fear of criticism, which can be as difficult as overcoming a fear of failure or conquering a fear of change. But it's a fact of life and in fact can come enervating. Fear of criticism results in several cerebral difficulties. Criticism, and the fear of it, robs us of self-regard, minimizes our particular action, crumbles our sense of acceptability and power, takes down self-reliance, and generates numerous other negative goods.

Criticism can be hard to take; it's little surprise that being hysterical about it in the plant is extremely common. But it's important to understand that criticism isn't the same as feedback. While both criticism and feedback involve evaluation, a crucial difference between feedback and criticism is that feedback is grounded on assessing and correcting information, whereas criticism is assessing and passing judgments and looking for faults. People may fear criticism for a variety of reasons. There are some common reasons

• Fear of failure. Criticism can feel like a particular attack and can be perceived as a failure. People may fear that criticism will confirm their worst fears about themselves or their capacities.

• Fear of rejection. Criticism can also feel like rejection, especially if it comes from someone whose opinion is largely valued. People may fear that criticism will lead to social or emotional rejection.

• Low self- regard. People with low self-regard may be more vulnerable to Criticism because they have a negative self-image and may believe that criticism confirms their negative beliefs about themselves.

• Perfectionism. People who strive for perfection may be more sensitive to criticism because they've high standards for themselves and may see criticism as substantiation that they've fallen short of those standards.

• Lack of experience. People who are new to a particular task or exertion may be more fearful of criticism because they warrant confidence in their capacities and may be more vulnerable to negative feedback.

• Cultural or family values. Some societies or families may place a high value on avoiding criticism or conflict, which can lead to a fear of criticism. Overcoming criticism when carrying out a difficult task can be gruelling, but there are strategies you can use to help you manage your fears and use feedback as a tool for growth and self-enhancement. There are some strategies to consider.

Step1.

Recognize your triggers. Identify the situations, people, or types of feedback that spark your fear of criticism. Understanding your triggers can help you anticipate and prepare for situations that may be particularly gruelling.

Step2.
Reframe criticism as feedback. Rather than viewing critics as a negative experience, wireframe it as feedback that can help you learn and grow. Try to view feedback as an occasion to ameliorate your skills and approach to the task.

Step3.
Seek out formative feedback. Rather than fearing criticism, seek out formative feedback from someone you trust and respect. Ask for their input on your approach and hear their suggestions with an open mind.

Step4.
Practice self-compassion. Be kind to yourself and admit that making miscalculations and facing critics is a natural part of the literacy process. Treat yourself with compassion and tolerance as you work through the task.

Step5.

Break the task down into lower, manageable steps. Breaking a difficult task down into lower, more manageable steps can help you feel less overwhelmed and more confident in your capability to complete it. Celebrate small successes along the way.

Step6.

Focus on your goals. Keep your attention on your goals and the reasons why you're bearing the difficult task. fantasize about yourself completing the task and achieving your goals.

Step7.

Make a support system. Compass yourself with people who are probative and encouraging. Having a support system can help you stay motivated and confident in your capacities.

Remember, managing the fear of criticism is a process and may take time and practice. By using these strategies and taking small steps towards your goals, you can build your confidence and overcome your fear of criticism when carrying out difficult tasks.

CHAPTER 7

PROCESS OF CARRYING OUT DIFFICULT TASKS FIRST.

Most successful and productive workers constantly put their most difficult tasks first ahead of lower tasks. Carrying out a difficult task can be a gruelling process, but it can also be satisfying and fulfilling. Then there are some general ways to consider when approaching a difficult task:

1. Define the task. launch by defining the task and understanding what's needed to complete it. Break

the task down into lower, more manageable ways, and prioritize these ways.

2. Plan and prepare. Develop a plan for completing the task, including timelines and resources needed. Gather any necessary accouterments and tools, and identify any implicit roadblocks or challenges that may arise.

3. Take action. Once you have a plan in place, take action and begin working on the task. Focus on one step at a time and try to stay present in the moment rather than getting overwhelmed by the big picture.

4. Examine progress. As you work on the task, cover your progress and acclimate your approach as demanded. Be open to feedback from others and consider any changes that may be necessary to ameliorate your approach.

5. Celebrate success. When you complete a step or reach a corner in the task, take time to admit your progress and celebrate your successes. This can help to boost your motivation and confidence as you move forward.

6. Reflect and learn. Once the task is complete, take time to reflect on your approach and what you learned from the experience. Consider what worked well and what you could do else in the future.

Remember, the process of carrying out a difficult task may vary depending on the task itself and your strengths and challenges. Use these ways as a general companion and acclimatize them to fit your specific situation. By breaking the task down into manageable ways, planning and preparing, taking action, covering progress, celebrating success, and reflecting on your experience, you can successfully carry out a difficult task.

CHAPTER 8

CARRY- OUT DIFFICULT TASKS FREQUENTLY.

POINT 1

CARRY- OUT DIFFICULT TASKS AROUND YOUR WORKSPACE.

POINT 2

CARRY- OUT DIFFICULT TASKS FOR YOUR FINANCE.

You need to carry out difficult tasks frequently to achieve your goals and be successful. Because the hard things eventually make you up and change your life. However, realize your mind is lying to you If you formerly feel like you're at the end of your rope moment with little slack left to hold on to. It has locked you by reciting self-defeating stories in your head — stories about your miscalculations and what you should have done else. And you've begun to believe that you're wedged. But you're NOT. You're alive in an immense world with horizonless destinations. Remember that adversity — doing and dealing with the hard things in life is the first path to variety. Your defeats frequently serve as well as your palms to shake your spirit and light your way. You just have to hold on tight, embrace the diurnal pain, and burn it as energy for your trip. Easier said than done, of course. This is why you need to continually remind yourself to always carry out difficult tasks frequently. Carrying out difficult tasks frequently can be a gruelling but satisfying experience. There are many reasons why.

1. Building adaptability. Taking on difficult tasks can help make adaptability, which is the capability to overcome adversity. The more you challenge yourself, the more you learn to bounce back from lapses and keep moving forward.

2. Develops new skills. Difficult tasks frequently cause you to learn new skills or improve existing ones. By pushing yourself to attack these challenges, you can develop your capacities and come more at handling analogous situations in the future.

3. Increases confidence. Completing a difficult task can give you a sense of accomplishment and boost your confidence. This can help you attack more gruelling tasks with lesser ease in the future.

4. Fosters growth. Taking on difficult tasks can help you grow professionally. By pushing yourself outside of your comfort zone, you can expand your knowledge and witness new things, leading to particular and professional growth.

CARRY- OUT DIFFICULT TASKS AROUND YOUR WORKSPACE.

Occasionally, a task is simply a commodity that you're not familiar with. Perhaps you don't know how to use the tools demanded for the task, or perhaps you're just not familiar with the process. To get over this challenge, proper exploration and training are necessary. Indeed the most introductory exploration can help you handle a difficult task. By doing exploration, you can acquire the knowledge, skill or gift needed of you. One illustration is print editing. numerous VAs are assigned to edit images and prints in connection with listing particulars on Amazon or social media marketing. Indeed without previous print editing knowledge, you can still negotiate this task by doing an exploration. With the vast resources available to you, there's no reason not to negotiate any task. Carrying out difficult tasks around your work can be a great way to challenge yourself and grow professionally. Here are some tips for taking on difficult tasks:

1. Set clear goals. Before starting a difficult task, make sure you have a clear understanding of what you are trying to achieve. Set specific, measurable goals that will help you track your progress and stay motivated.

2. Break it down. Difficult tasks can frequently feel inviting, so break them down into lower, more

manageable ways. This will make the task feel less daunting and help you stay focused on the individual factors.

3. Prioritize. Make sure you are fastening on the most critical tasks first, and also move on to the further gruelling task.

4. Seek help. Do not be hysterical to ask for help or advice when you are faced with a difficult task. Reach out to associates, instructors, or indeed online communities to get the support you need.

5. Stay positive. It's important to maintain a positive attitude when faced with a difficult task. Focus on your strengths and successes, and use them as motivation to attack the challenge ahead.

Remember, taking on difficult tasks around your work can be gruelling, but it can also be incredibly satisfying. Embrace the challenge, stay focused, and do not be hysterical to ask for help when you need it.

CARRY- OUT DIFFICULT TASKS FOR YOUR FINANCE.

Managing your finances can be a gruelling task, especially if you are facing financial difficulties or have limited resources. Still, taking a way to ameliorate your fiscal situation can pay off in the long run, and frequently requires doing hard things that might feel dispiriting at first. By making tough opinions, setting goals, and staying chastened, you can achieve financial stability and make a better future for yourself and your loved ones. In this discussion, we will explore some of the difficult tasks you can do for your finances, and how they can help you ameliorate your fiscal situation over time. Yes, doing difficult tasks can be necessary for achieving your fiscal goals. This can involve making offerings, being chastened, and taking calculated risks. There are some examples of difficult tasks you might need to do to achieve your fiscal goals.

1. Cut back on expenses. If you want to save further money, you may need to cut back on certain

expenses, similar to eating out or buying precious clothes.

2. Work redundant hours. If you want to increase your income, you may need to work redundant hours or take on a side hustle.

3. Invest in yourself. If you want to advance your career and earn more money in the long run, you may need to invest in yourself by getting fresh education or training.

4. Take a calculated risk. Investing in the stock request or starting your own business can be parlous, but it can also lead to significant fiscal prices.

Remember that achieving fiscal goals can take time and trouble, and there may be lapses along the way. Still, by doing hard things and staying married to your goals, you can increase your chances of achieving financial success.

CHAPTER 9

FINAL CONCLUSIONS ON CARRYING OUT DIFFICULT TASKS FIRST.

In my experience, doing the most difficult task first is a precious habit to develop. By dividing difficult tasks beforehand, you can free up internal energy and concentrate on other important liabilities. This approach can help you avoid procrastination, reduce stress and anxiety, and increase your overall productivity.   Of course, it's not always easy to prioritize the hard things, especially when they feel inviting or unwelcome. Still, there are strategies you can use to make it more manageable, similar as breaking down the task into a lower, more manageable way, setting realistic goals and deadlines, and seeking support or guidance from others when demanded.   Eventually, the key to success is thickness and continuity. By making a habit of prioritizing the hard things, you can develop less discipline and adaptability, which will serve you well in all areas of your life. So, if you are looking to ameliorate your productivity, reduce stress, and achieve your goals, consider committing to doing the most difficult task first.

www.ingramcontent.com/pod-product-compliance
Lightning Source LLC
Chambersburg PA
CBHW071145220526
45467CB00015B/1960